HELP!

My Feelings are sticking out of my gown!

Author: Maurie Shapiro-Comenzo, PhD, LPC, ABCAC
Co-author & Illustrator: Jordyn Shapiro

Dear James & Kim,

Thanks for the laughter and support!

I got your behind... I mean your back, anytime

 Jordyn

About the Author

Maurie Shapiro-Comenzo, Ph.D., LPC

As a recognized relationship and life skills expert, Maurie serves in private practice and Adjunct Professor in Phoenix, Arizona.

For over 20 years she has specialized in group, family and individual psychotherapy
addressing the dynamics of coping with life controlling challenges.

Maurie engages, energizes and inspires her audiences and counselees while providing empathy and genuine compassion.

About the Co-Author

Jordyn Shapiro is a junior at NYIT University majoring in Art & Computer Graphics. She is a 2007 recipient of the UCB Crohn's $10,000 scholarship for her academic achievements and perseverance through her disease.

She is co-founder of The Foundation for Nutrition and Inflammatory Bowel Diseases In Children, Inc., (NIBD). NIBD was formed to raise awareness and foster further research in nutrition and growth factor interventions currently available to patients with IBD. You can learn more about NIBD and Jordyn at www.nibdinkids.com
The cover picture of this workbook is my representation of how people feel vulnerable when faced with a diagnosis of disease. Nobody feels good wearing this and the gown for me emphasizes my illness on display.

The collage of feelings is all the thoughts crowding my mind when I ALLOW my disease to invade my thoughts! "Don't give your illness the power, try and focus on the positive!"

Love,
Jordyn

A note to the Facilitator:

Please feel free to apply the tools and workbook activities in the order you believe is most appropriate. You may follow the format from cover to cover.
However, if a particular life situation is most applicable, feel free to utilize its value based on a specific topic.

I would welcome any feedback you wish to share.

Contact:
Dr. Maurie Shapiro-Comenzo
C/o NIBD
354 N. Iowa Avenue
N. Massapequa, NY 11758
Email: nibdinkids@aol.com

Healing wounded hearts together!
Maurie

Dear Therapist, Medical Professional, Parent, Adult Facilitator:

As you may have already encountered watching a young person, or adult experience the physical and emotional pain of having to cope with illness, injury or significant challenges, demanding a total life change is very difficult. We may objectively know the clinical/ medical interventions required. Yet, the actual day to day living, suffering, having the medical issues dictate the way one must accept life in this season is indescribable.

For the identified child the experience of having to face losing the ability to make free choices "What I want to do today?" through the denial of startling limitations out of one's control is far beyond what the average person will ever experience in a life time.

The process of moving through the stages of fear, dread, anger and resentment, blame and frustration, sadness, loneliness, are just a few extreme emotions a patient experiences. Having to give up and face loss of how one originally lived daily is beyond the average person's perception. I believe that these stages of adjustment are comparable to those in the stages of grief and loss. For the patient it is the death of a vision of self, life that was once predictable and familiar is shattered with no end in sight. The natural effort one desperately attempts to make in order to gain some sense of order is out of reach. For these children, the world as they once knew is gone. Their self-esteem and identity is pulled out from under them! An individuals's societal value is based on performance and achievement especially in academics, sports or the arts. The world's measuring stick of success determines one's success, as unhealthy

6

as that is, even children gain a sense of self value on whether or not they fit in to the societal norm.

In order to facilitate the process of working through this workbook, one must keep these challenging, painful experiences in mind. Anger may be the observed behavior. Yet, for children learning how to identify and express emotions is critical for their emotional adjustment. Anger most often masks other genuine feelings. The child may not know how to express these feelings. The way in which you and the family handle the emotions will add to or hinder the child's willingness to safely discover, identify and ultimately learn appropriate ways to express and resolve emotions and personal conflicts.

The adults in the child's life must be willing to encourage this process. Children need to know that they have the approval and "permission" to work through these stages of healing.

Several times, throughout the lessons, it is strongly emphasized that feelings aren't "right or wrong". What we do with those feelings will determine whether one is "right or wrong".

They need permission to make mistakes, blow up out of frustration and feel the natural feeling of self-pity and lack of self-esteem in the process of rediscovering self-worth.

As mentioned before, the very ways in which a child, or adult, measures internal accomplishment is based on the approval of peers, authority figures and the key individuals in the child's life. We must remember the grief and extreme loss each individual faces when physical challenges hinder them from feeling "good enough", accepted, special and accomplished. The areas that were once successful within their "measuring stick" process, no longer appear a positive alternative.

The bottom line is the child must receive the message from those they seek approval from, that "You have a Right to feel sad, angry, jealous, disappointed etc." Validate the truth of their current reality by confirming and saying "I understand for now you can no longer do the things you did before, BUT together we can learn some new ways to make you shine". Emphasize that he/she is not alone. There are so many other important ways a person can measure personal accomplishment. Focus on the character of the child, inner strengths and talents.

The choices which form an individual's character ultimately, we must rethink in our "measuring stick". A marvelous professional, in the Mental Health field states, "We need to focus on What's Strong not Wrong!" (Ann MacNeil, Phoenix, AZ)

Our transitional shift begins with acceptance that the child has these limitations but we will not allow those limitations to hinder how the child views him or herself.

Parents, as well as all of the significant others in a child's life, must focus on character strengths. We need to teach the significant adults, in the child's life, the value of many topics in this workbook. The whole family can become excited about "Acts of Kindness", "Your Message to the World", "Creating Collages of Feelings", "Wishes and Dreams", or designing their own awesome "Super

Powers Person". Together, we can help each child gain character strengths, increase positive life values and the imperative qualities necessary in order to be a magnificent human being.

In spite of their limitations, hope can be re-ignited! Each child or adolescent can regain a sense of self-worth and dignity. Together, we can help them soar!

Respectfully with unending hope,
Maurie

The Purpose: Directed to the Professionals, Parents and Loved Ones

- To validate the client/patient/your child's experiences which may result in disappointment, discouragement, leading to anger, depression and hopelessness.

- To teach the client/patient/your child how to recognize those feelings and learn how to express them in a healthy way.

- To assist the client/patient/your child in the process of discovering, communicating and successfully resolving the common challenges they face.

- To bring hope and encouragement, through the intervention activities, that will lead to enhancement of self-esteem.

- To help the client/patient/your child explore new opportunities, in spite of his/her limitations. This serves as the catalyst for facilitating new dreams and personal development.

- To provide expressive therapeutic experiences that facilitates a healthier internalized view of self. As they work through the learning activities he/she shifts from thoughts saying

- "I'm no longer capable of doing"…to realizing, "I can do wonderful things with the gifts and talents I still have." The client/patient/your child discovers that, by having a renewed self-perception, confidence and courage are reignited.

- The client/patient/your child shifts from focusing on his/her losses and limitations to a more hopeful, renewed positive self-view.

- When the workbook is completed and comments are made by the client/patient/your child such as:

- "There are some cool things I can DO!"

- "I have gifts and talents that I can use to be whatever I want to be!"

- "I have been inspired and heartened as I see YOU move forward with a new sense of hope and excitement."

Message to Professionals, Parents and Love Ones:

No matter what age a person is, one gains a sense of identity through the perception of life experiences. We gradually discover where our self-worth and confidence is.

We begin to know who we are! Our ability to adapt to societal norms, family values, combined with the impact of personal experiences can sometimes cause us to doubt our sense of stability and identity.

When all is said and done, one thing is for sure. If faced with a tragedy, whether it is sudden physical limitations, pain that may develop into unbearable pain or a situation that overwhelms us, our actions depend on our "Life Instructors". These "Life Instructors" include parents, teachers, strong significant others, extended family, physicians, nurses, social workers etc.

Each of these valuable dynamics has an internal message which becomes engraved in our hearts. In addition to lots of ideas of what's right, wrong, good, bad, tolerable, unacceptable, we have many other pieces of our life puzzle to cope with.

"This is what I think about life and who I am somehow grows within us as each of these significant people and messages we conclude, impact the way we will cope or not cope with life's negative challenges." As certain aspects of our lives become more predictable or unpredictable, life can be extremely challenging. The unknown can be frightening, depending on our values, faith, and the tools we have gained for coping with life.

12

Throughout my research and years of practice and experience as an Expressive Intervention Specialist, I continue to meet families facing many of the issues in this workbook. My courageous niece, Jordyn, was the inspiration for developing these activities and expressive intervention tools. Through her willingness to share the challenges that repeatedly arose, as she adjusted to her illness, came to be. With the most positive persevering outlook she has managed her physical needs and progressive limitations that became more difficult to cope with in the school setting. As a result, she soon became homebound and isolated.

I, too, experienced a life changing event which resulted in my having to be homebound and frequently bedridden for approximately two years. The range of emotions that were directly related to my illness forced me to accept abrupt changes that I had no control over. Things we all take for granted were no longer there to depend on. The most difficult adjustment for me was the sudden loss of control I had over my own life. I remember saying, "I feel like I died and woke up in someone else's body and life."

As experienced by all patients having to face many physical and emotional challenges, one is desperate to have the life they once had returned to them. One loses independence and the ability to be self-reliant. At any age strength and predictability is stripped away as a result of having physical challenges.

Jordyn and I, though at separate times and in different ways, experienced similar emotional reactions and responses to our physical limitations and challenges.

How Jordyn and I Changed Our Focus

When Jordyn first became sick, she and I would talk on the phone about lots of things.

One day she asked me how I managed to get through my own physical challenges when I was very sick and homebound. As we continued to share our thoughts and ideas, Jordyn began to Discover things that she could do while she was sick.

It was very difficult for her when she had to stop participating in the activities she used to love!

Giving up dancing, karate and skiing to name a few!

Sometimes we talked about how it feels to be sick every day, our worries and how people treat us or look at us differently. We came up with lots of fun things that helped to keep our minds focused on good, positive things instead of all the disappointments.

The Purpose of This Workbook:
Directed to the Client/Patient/Your Child

*To remind you that you are not alone as a young person facing challenges.
 Lots of kids and teens are out there struggling with many of the same problems
  that you are.

*To encourage you when you are facing days or nights that become challenging.

*To provide tools for change in order to feel happier and
  positive when faced with life changing situations.

*No matter whom you are or where you are at with your challenges, there is always HOPE!

We can keep holding on to that hope for one another!

Table of Contents

In each of the following chapters you and your client or child will have the opportunity to Identify, Express and Resolve the challenging issues faced on a daily basis through these helpful activities.

Chapter 1:
Anger

Do You Ever Just Want to Yell and Scream?

One time Jordyn said, "I get so tired of being sick, having pain and just not feeling well.

It makes me want to scream!"

Do you ever feel anger and disappointment?

When someone doesn't feel well, everyday can be challenging. A person may feel too sick to go out and play. That can be very disappointing.

I miss out on all the fun with my friends and family
At times, I get bored and lonely! Why is this happening again?
I can't wait until I feel better.

Jordyn expressed her anger and disappointment by drawing the pictures on the next pages.

Do you see any pictures that remind you of how you think or feel sometimes?

What might the people in the pictures be saying?
You can draw your own Anger picture:
Remember it's your picture! Whatever you draw is perfect and really helps to get your feelings out and on paper.

Draw Here:

Repeat these words 2 to 3 times:

"It's OK to feel what I feel but what I do about the feeling can become right or wrong."

As you think about this is there anything you would like to change, do or say differently?

Talk with someone about how you might set a goal for this. Example: you might realize that you have a mean attitude when you don't feel well.

This may cause you to speak to others in a rude or unkind manner. We never like someone else to treat us rudely when they don't feel well.

So, it should not be okay to behave that way toward other people. Talk about how you might change this and write some ideas down

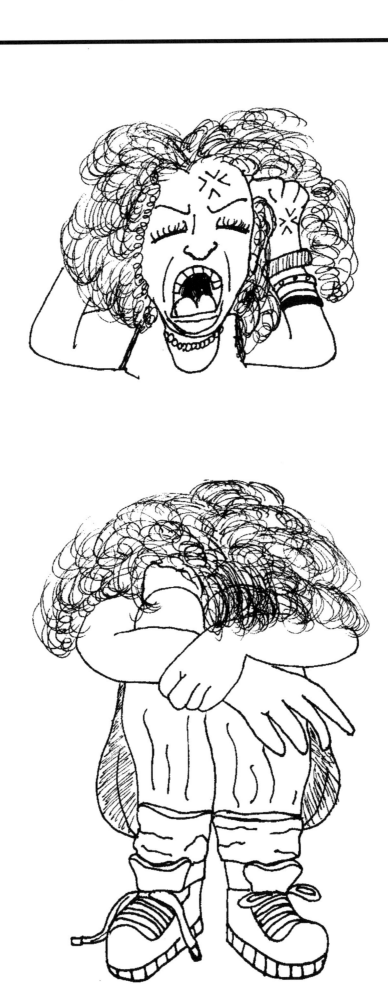

Chapter 2:
A Collage of
My Feelings

My Collage of Feelings

A note from Jordyn: "At first, I didn't want to create a collage. I never tried to make one before.

Once I began, I caught myself saying a negative self-talk statement. I said, I don't like this!

I don't want to make a collage and I don't know how!" Then I tried to come up with positive Self-talk, I said, "I have never tried this. I can make this a cool adventure and look for words message to the people who will see it!" Afterwards, I started to get excited as I looked through magazine pictures and words.

You can begin by looking through different kinds of magazines. Cut out anything you see that describes what you think, what you believe, how you feel or anything that is a word or picture of things you like, places you enjoy or anything you wish! "Sometimes, I get really tired of being sick. I just want to SCREAM. Do you feel that way?"(Jordyn)
After your collage is finished check out Jordyn's.

How to Describe Your Collage to Others

Try to share how the following feelings or thoughts may have occurred.

How did you choose the words and pictures?

What feelings do those words and pictures express?

Describe what the experience was like as you created the collage?

Describe how you felt after you completed the collage?

Remember: We never have to compare our pictures, drawings or any artistic creations with anyone else's. Yours will be perfect because you are the expert about yourself, your feelings, thoughts and your creations.

Draw Here:

This is all my thoughts crowding my mind when I ALLOW my disease to invade my thoughts! Don't give your illness the power, try and focus on the positive!

Chapter 3: Feelings as Seasons Pass

As Seasons Pass By

Do you sometimes feel left out like everyone and everything is going on without you?

Example: Think about do you spend a lot of your days trying to recuperate from your last set back?

Have you ever wished you had someone else's body?

(Jordyn and I each experienced this in different ways!)

Try to draw a picture, write or talk about this with someone.
Write down what you would say about this:
What seasons do you like the most?
What things about each season do you find yourself missing?
Try to draw a picture that makes you smile about each of your favorite seasons.
Think of something you could do when you can't do some of your favorite season activities.
Start with one season at a time and use your imagination.

Example: You may draw a huge snowman as your winter picture. Make sure to ask for lots of ideas!

"Sometimes I feel a lot of emotions at the same time! When I get my hopes up and hope that by next Spring I will be well enough to do some things I haven't been well enough to do. Then, I get really sad and angry that I still am not well enough to do those things I was hoping for."

What might you be thinking or feeling if you were the boy or girl in these pictures?

Write or talk about it.

_____

_____

_____

_____

_____

_____

_____

_____

_____

Draw Here:

Chapter 4: Talking about My Feelings

Talking About My Feelings

When someone doesn't feel well, every day can be extremely challenging.

A person may feel too sick to go out and play.
Disappointment can happen often when your feeling sick.
Example: Someone may say: "Sometimes I feel sad and angry when I don't feel well enough to go somewhere I really wanted to."
When I can't do fun things, I used to do, I get bored or lonely.
I might ask myself **"Why is this happening?"**

It helps when I talk about my thoughts and feelings with someone I trust.

Who do you like to talk to when you don't feel well or when you're going through a hard time because of your challenges?

What feelings or thoughts do you experience?

Learning More About Feelings & How to Cope with Them

On the next page you can look at lots of **feelings** people have also called **emotions**.

What feelings do you have sometimes?

Take some time to check off the feelings/emotions that you experience.

When you finish listing your feelings write about what you can do to help yourself.

Describe a coping activity or tool you can use to handle the feeling.

_____

_____

_____

_____

_____

_____

_____

eMotioNs

aggressive	alienated	angry	annoyed	anxious	apathetic	bashful
bored	cautious	confident	confused	curious	depressed	determined
disappointed	discouraged	disgusted	embarrassed	enthusiastic	envious	ecstatic
excited	exhausted	fearful	frightened	frustrated	guilty	happy
helpless	hopeful	hostile	humiliated	hurt	hysterical	innocent
interested	jealous	lonely	loved	lovestruck	mischievous	miserable
negative	optimistic	pained	paranoid	peaceful	proud	puzzled
regretful	relieved	sad	satisfied	shocked	shy	sorry
stubborn	sure	surprised	suspicious	thoughtful	undecided	withdrawn

Example:
"Sometimes I feel sad that I can't do what other kids, my age are doing."

"How can I help myself?

What activity/tool can I use to help me?

I will use the activity/ tool of focusing on the positive.

Make a list of the things you can still do.

Describe how you can do one of those things when you want to feel happier.

_____

_____

_____

_____

_____

_____

_____

Chapter 5: Roller Coaster Feelings

Roller Coaster Feelings

Remember when we learned that feelings and thoughts are most common when you face challenges?
This next part of our book will help you when your feelings go up, down and all around,
Just like a roller coaster!

Remember:
Feelings are always okay.
What you do with a negative feeling or thought makes all the difference!
The choice is yours to do the right thing with your feelings.

It is also important to remember when you are not feeling well, or coping with physical challenges, it never gives us the right to hurt someone else.

This may happen when we, with our words or actions, take our hurts and frustrations out on others around us. (Especially when they are just trying to help.)

THAT IS NOT OKAY.

Yes, you are trying to cope with a lot of issues and challenges, yet the people who try to help you are working very hard as well.
Don't forget that they are hurting too.
It hurts to see someone you love or care about in so much discomfort and pain.

Do you ever feel like you have many different feelings all at the same time?

It sometimes feels like you want to explode, cry or just tear something up!

Remember, it's always okay to feel what you feel but how you handle the feelings are very important.

Name the different feelings you see in this picture.

The Emotional Rollercoaster

Try to add your own pictures of people and their "roller coaster feelings"

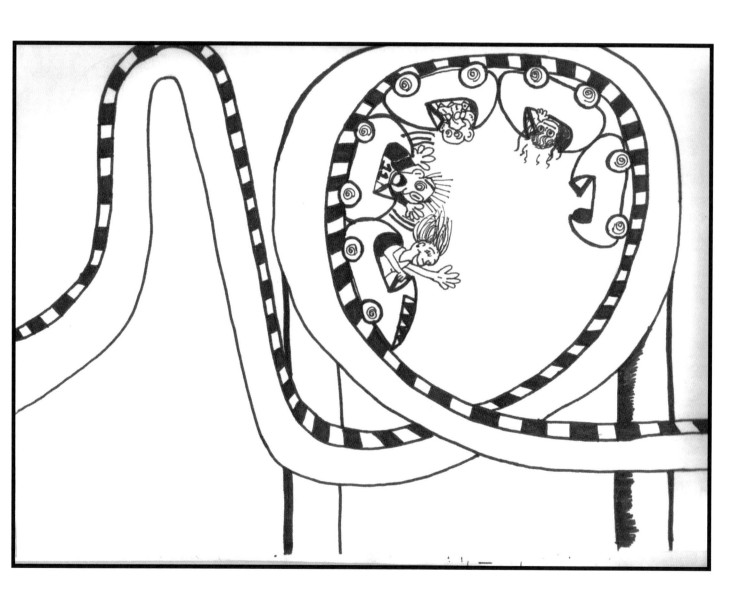

Draw Here:

Chapter 6:
Self Talk

Self-Talk

Self -talk is about the things people tell themselves.
Most people are negative self-talkers, which means they are really good at putting themselves down.

Everyone has "Self-Talk" and many people don't even realize the things they say in their self-talk.

My counselor taught me that most people say negative things to themselves.

People need to learn about the positive things to tell themselves.
It takes practice, but it is a gift to ourselves every time we remind ourselves to focus on something positive.

Example: When I don't think about my self-talk, I sometimes say to myself:

"I'm such a loser! Then I catch myself saying that and remind myself, I'm really good at art. I love having more time to draw."
That's Positive Self-Talk!

At first, I was surprised at how many times I told myself negative things. It just took practice to turn a negative thought or feeling around.

It is important to know that it's okay to feel sad, angry, totally frustrated or any feeling. Those are natural feelings!

44

How to turn your Self-Talk around:

A person my get in the habit of negative self-talk. Instead of repeating those thoughts and feelings over again, we can try looking at anything positive.

Examples of Negative and Positive Self-Talk

"I am angry that I have to go to a new doctor again!"
"I am a loser! Nothing ever goes my way.

Let's now change that into a positive statement
"I am angry. That's okay, but I am not a loser!"
"I am brave and courageous and will have my parent(s) with me to feel safe."
"I don't have to be afraid. I realize I am feeling scared and angry."

It is your turn to listen to the negative things you tell yourself, sometimes.
What negative thoughts or feelings do you say to yourself?

_____

_____

_____

_____

Make a list of what you're beginning to realize in your own Self-Talk:

_____

_____

_____

_____

What positive thoughts or feelings can you tell yourself instead?

_____

_____

_____

_____

Now write something you can practice saying to yourself as positive Self-Talk
*ask someone for ideas, you may be surprised!

Examples of Positive Self-Talk:

"I am not alone. There are others who have it worse than I do."
"I choose to be thankful for what I have, like my supportive family and doctors.
"Tomorrow will be a better day."

Remember : **It's always okay to feel and think the way you do. What we do with those feelings and thoughts is the most important part.**

Make a choice to try using a new activity or tool in order to make positive changes in your life.

Draw or color, even doodle, it will help to get your mind off your situation. Write about your feelings in a poem or putting your words to music. Listen to music. Talk about your feelings with someone you trust.

It's Your Turn to Practice Listening to What You Tell Yourself

You probably don't even realize when you do it. It's your turn to listen more to negative things you tell yourself.

What's going on inside? It's very important for you to give yourself permission to express those thoughts and feelings.

We need to learn to recognize situations that trigger and cause us to feel or think negatively.

Make a list of situations that may cause you to begin feeling or thinking negatively:

Causes and Triggers	**Thoughts I'm Thinking**
_____	_____
_____	_____
_____	_____
_____	_____
_____	_____
_____	_____
_____	_____

Go Back to your list. What can you do to feel better?:
Try to think of new ways to respond to causes and triggers, and how I can respond more positively.

_____

_____

_____

Fill in the Blanks Activity:
Negative thoughts and feelings I tell myself:
Think of a time when things didn't go the way you were hoping they would.

A time my feelings were hurt

_____

What happened?

_____

I told my self...

_____

Now try to change the negative thought to something positive.

A time when things didn't go as I hoped they would:

What happened?

_____

How were you hoping things would go?

_____

How did things turn out instead?

_____

When you try to listen to what you felt or told yourself, what do you remember?

_____

What positive things could you tell yourself if the situation happened again?

_____

First always remember that, "it's okay to feel the way we feel." We want to change the way we react to our feelings. We never want to hurt ourselves or others because of a feeling.
Even though you're still feeling that negative feeling begin to practice positive words and thoughts. (Your doing great!)

Chapter 7:
Your
Message to
the World

Your Message to the World

Sometimes we wish we could help people understand what it is like not to feel well all of the time.

Pretend you are on a mountain top and you have a special microphone to tell someone or many people, or the whole wide world your message.

What would you say or do?

_____

_____

_____

_____

Perhaps you can teach the people around you "What helps you? Or "What you need?"- especially when you're feeling sad, angry, or worried.

<u>Whether it is a small or giant feeling, teach the people in your world how they can support you.</u>

_____

_____

_____

_____

How would you write or speak about your own message to the world:

Take your time.

Use your imagination to think of anything and everything you would really like to say.

Start by making a list of whatever comes to mind.

You may start with the following ideas:

When I don't feel well or in pain I think…
When I'm having a hard day I feel like…
When I'm in pain or having a challenging day, what I need is…
What helps me the most is when you…

Now add as many of your own ideas that you want.

_____

_____

_____

_____

_____

_____

_____

Chapter 8:
Acts of
Kindness

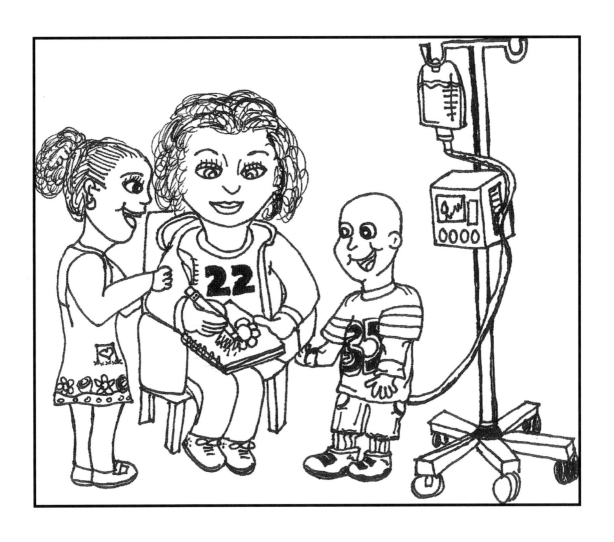

Acts of Kindness

What is an Act of Kindness?

An act of kindness is when we do something for someone just to be kind. We do these with the attitude of giving and not expecting something in return. Especially when we surprise a person with an act of kindness, it will make the person feel special and important!

Ideas for Acts of Kindness:

You can call or text a person and say, "I was just thinking about you!"

You can send a hand-made card or note to cheer someone up who is not feeling well.

This shows someone you care about them!

Doing Things for Others:

Even when we don't feel well, it's important to try doing things to get our minds off our own challenges and reach out to another person who is not feeling well or going through a difficult time.

It will help you to feel better when you begin thinking of fun ways to make someone else's day better!

Take some time to check off all of the feelings that you feel sometimes or all the time. You may want to look at the feelings pictures again.

What It's Like on the Other Side

Have you ever tried to help a friend who seemed unhappy? Maybe you ask, "What's wrong?" The person said, "Nothing!" You know that is not true, but you also can tell that the person doesn't want to talk.

How does that make you feel?

_____

_____

Talk or write about how it feels or what you think when you have tried to help someone else that seems unhappy.

Try to accept that the person feels that way. A good friend realizes that it is Okay if someone else chooses to have some quiet, thinking time.

Our way is not necessarily the only way or the right way.

eMotiONs

aggressive	alienated	angry	annoyed	anxious	apathetic	bashful
bored	cautious	confident	confused	curious	depressed	determined
disappointed	discouraged	disgusted	embarrassed	enthusiastic	envious	ecstatic
excited	exhausted	fearful	frightened	frustrated	guilty	happy
helpless	hopeful	hostile	humiliated	hurt	hysterical	innocent
interested	jealous	lonely	loved	lovestruck	mischievous	miserable
negative	optimistic	pained	paranoid	peaceful	proud	puzzled
regretful	relieved	sad	satisfied	shocked	shy	sorry
stubborn	sure	surprised	suspicious	thoughtful	undecided	withdrawn

How to be a good friend:

Even when we think someone would feel better by talking about what is bothering them, we need to accept the fact he/she doesn't want to talk, right now.

A good friend lets a person be free to talk when he/she wants to. Instead of trying to force someone to do something our way, we need to respect other people's thoughts and feelings.
We can teach the people in our lives what we need and how to help us!

Chapter 9: Coping with Changes

Coping with Changes

Jordyn shared: "When my sister, Skylar and I were younger we joined a dance class each school year. When I began to feel too sick to dance anymore it was very disappointing for both of us. Sometimes I felt sad and guilty when my sister started dancing without me.

I didn't want my sister to feel guilty or sad because she could still participate in dance classes and recitals. Before I got sick we had pictures taken of us in our dance recital costumes.
After I got sick our special dance pictures were of her alone. That was hard for both of us."

Our physical challenges can cause changes for ourselves and others.

_____

_____

_____

Do you ever have that experience?

_____

_____

_____

_____

_____

What is it like for you?

_____

_____

_____

_____

What thoughts and feelings do you experience?

_____

_____

_____

_____

It is natural for people to dislike change. Change can be difficult for everyone. We don't know what the change will bring or take from our lives. When we share our thoughts and feelings with a safe person, we may feel better.

How Can You Practice Coping with Changes

What can you tell yourself if this happens to you? *(Try using Positive Self-Talk)

Complete this sentence:

It always helps me feel better when I tell myself...

What changes do you see in these pictures?

64

Example: I can tell myself, "Tomorrow will be a better day!"

Draw a picture of what your better day will look like.

What changes do you experience?

_____

_____

_____

_____

_____

_____

_____

_____

_____

_____

Draw Here:

Chapter 10:
Changing
Our Focus

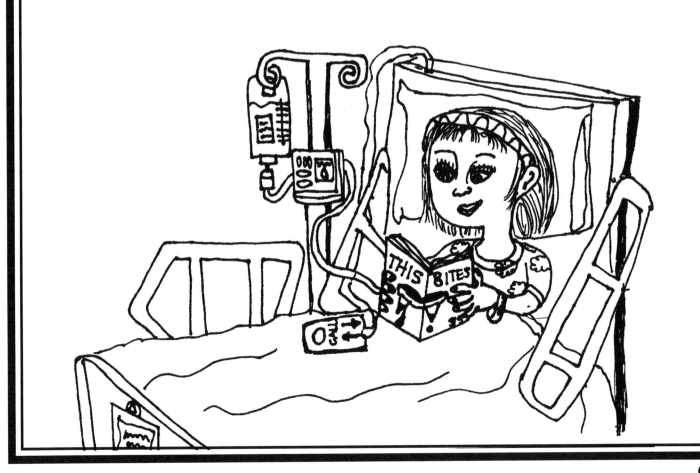

Changing Our Focus

Sometimes it is really difficult to get our minds off of how we are feeling. It helps to focus on something else.

What do you do in order to focus on something more positive?

When you are having a difficult or challenging day, what things can you do to focus on a positive thing?

What ideas can you come up with when you need to focus on something positive?

Write about it, draw or talk to someone in order to express what this is like for you.

<u>Next, draw a picture or write something that helps you feel better.</u>
<u>Example: Sometimes Jordyn likes to play computer games.</u>

Draw Here:

Changing Our Focus

Listening to music is a great way to change our focus.
What encouraging song, CD or positive message do you thing he is focused on?

_____

_____

_____

_____

_____

_____

<u>*What book would you like to read about when you want to focus on*</u>
<u>*something positive?*</u>

_____

_____

_____

_____

_____

_____

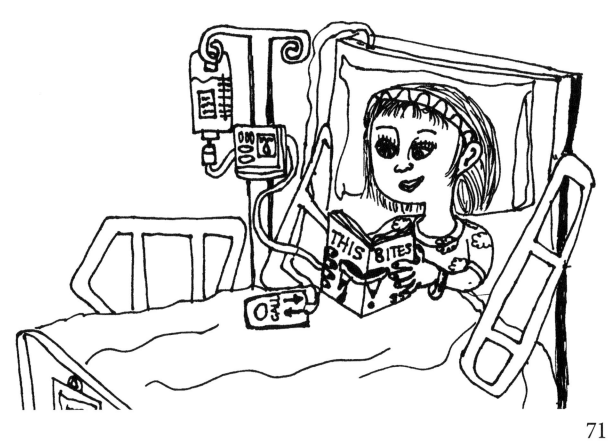

Chapter 11:
Designing
Your
Superpower
Person

Designing Your "Superpower Person"

Jordyn says: "Sometimes I imagine that I have superpowers! The superpowers would allow me to be and do all the things I don't always feel well enough to do."

Try to imagine what it would be like to create your own Superpower Person.

If you could imagine that you have Superpowers the following statements will help develop your imagination creation!
Start by completing the next sentences:

I would feel…
(Example: strong, invincible)

_____

_____

I would be able to…

_____

_____

I would begin to start…
(Example: helping animals, people)

_____

_____

My life would be…
(Example: awesome, helpful, give a voice)

_____

_____

People would…
(Example: listen, share)

_____

_____

My family would…
(Example: be so proud)

_____

_____

Add any ideas of your own!

_____

_____

_____

_____

_____

_____

My "Superpower Person Story"

Wow! Write a story about your Superpower Person.
Use your completed sentences to help you.
You may write the title before or after your story.

If someone else is joining you ask the following questions to help you get started.

What does my Superpower Person do to help others?

_____

_____

How does he/she help others?

_____

_____

What does he/she believe are some problems they wish to solve?

_____

_____

What makes each of them work so well together?

_____

_____

_____

Here is what I look like with my SUPERPOWERS:

You can draw or use magazine pictures and words.

Have Fun!!

(Idea: You might ask another person or several people to create a special Superpower Person of their own.)

Draw Here:

Band aid girl has the power to heal!

Chapter 12: Wishes and Dreams

Wishes and Dreams

"Sometimes I close my eyes and picture the night sky.
I can see all of the bright twinkling stars in my imaginary sky.
I might just make a wish upon a star this time…"

"My wish is for a cure for all disease and illness."…Jordyn xo

How would you complete the following wishes?

"Star light, star bright, here's the wish I wish tonight for…

My self

_____

_____

My family

_____

_____

My friends

_____

_____

My teachers

_____

_____

My doctor(s)

_____

_____

My nurses

_____

_____

The world

_____

_____

Turn to next Page...

Wishes and Dreams Activity:

Jordyn imagines herself on the ski slopes when she feels good!

Use your imagination to take you to an imaginary place.

Jordyn imagined herself being able to ski again!

Draw a picture or talk about what your imaginary day might look like?

Where would you go?

_____

_____

Who could come with you?

_____

_____

What rules might you put in place?

_____

_____

_____

_____

Draw Here:

Draw Here:

Chapter 13: Cares and Worries

Cares and Worries

Whenever I feel worried and scared I have a special place to put my feelings!
I take my cares and worries (i.e. something that I may be afraid of doing)

Write them on a piece of paper then crumple and crunch the paper up!

Finally, I put the paper in a special box and I say:

"I am going to take my cares and worries and put them here to stay."

Make your own special Cares and Worries box:

Think about what cares and worries you could put inside your own box!

You can use any box (shoe/cereal box)
Cover the box with plain paper
You can use pictures from magazines, words or draw your own.
Decorate the box anyway you like!
Label the box: "My Cares and Worries Box"
Write any worries on a piece of paper and place in the box.

Remember, follow the Cares and Worries Statement:
"I'm going to take my cares and worries…"

Example: If I put the feeling of "fear" in the box, what positive feeling would I exchange it for?

The opposite feeling of "fear", for me is "trust", also "safe".

I like to think that if I put that feeling in the box, I don't have to carry it around anymore. Instead I can carry whatever positive feeling I exchanged it for!

You can make your own design!

Draw Here:

Chapter 14:
Finding Comfort

Finding Comfort

Jordyn said:

"Sometimes, I just need some comfort.

For me, that can be asking for a hug or hugging my pet.

My dog comforts me."

Draw a picture or write about what comforts you!

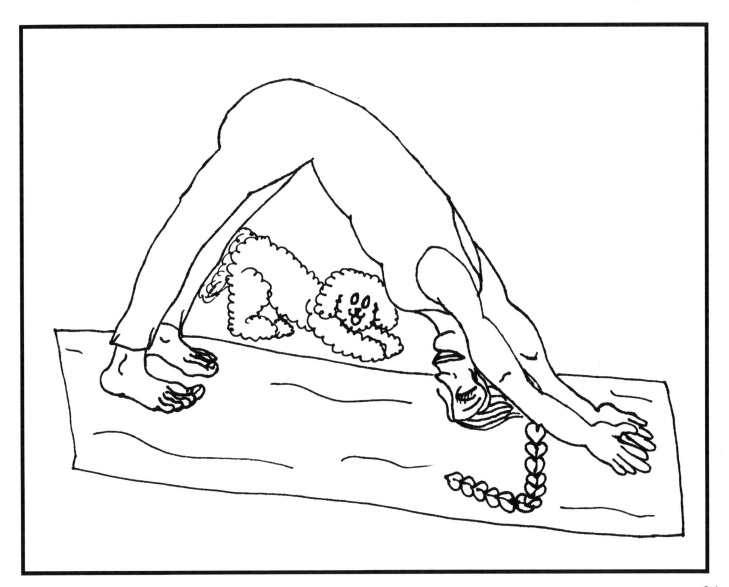

Draw Here:

Chapter 15:
Coping with
Lab and
Hospital Visits

Coping with Lab and Hospital Visits

When Jordyn first started going for repeated medical procedures she felt scared. At first it was very stressful just thinking about the next time she would need to go.

Jordyn discovered that if she listened to a relaxation tape or soft music, right before her visit, it helped her to relax and feel calmer. After a while she wasn't afraid anymore.

Each time Jordyn returned to the lab she noticed that there were other kids who looked scared!

One day Jordyn was drawing. She began to reach out to a young child by drawing a picture. As more kids began to see her art work, she began to receive requests to draw pictures of their favorite characters.

Drawing for those other patients allowed Jordyn to feel better. The other patients felt better too!

She realized that, by trying to distract other patients with her art work, she felt much happier.

Even now, each time Jordyn returns to that lab, she enjoys drawing for young patients. It also brings her a great feeling that we all experience when we help others during a challenging time.

Jordyn began using her talent to bring smiles to the children's faces! It made her feel better knowing she was helping others.

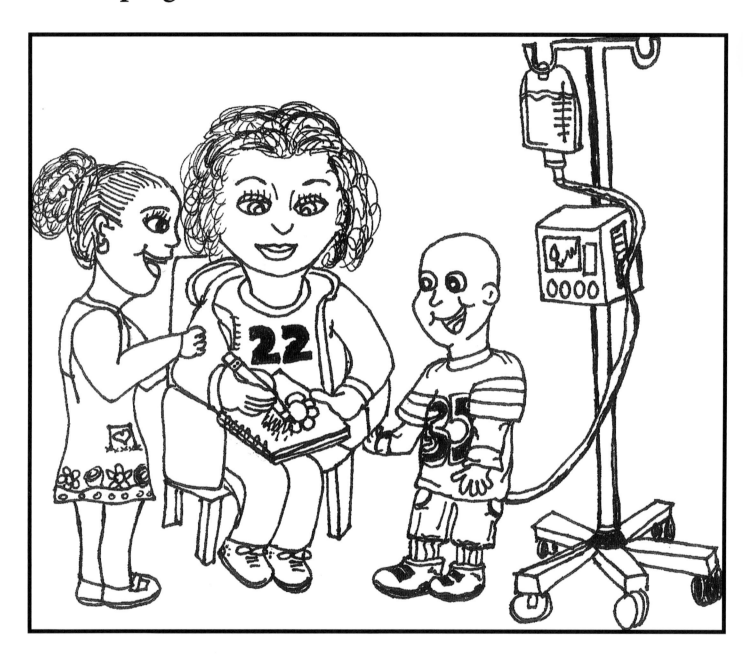

What talent can you do to possibly bring smiles to others that were once in your situation?

Draw it on the next page!

Draw Here:

Chapter 16: Special People who Try to Help You

Special People Who Try to Help You

Even though you are not feeling well, it is important to have an **"attitude of gratitude."**

An **attitude of gratitude** *is when you begin to be thankful for the people who try to help you. When you begin to focus on that, you can feel much better.*

Jordyn began to draw pictures of the special medical professionals who helped her.

She realized that each one of them had made an amazing difference in her life!

Make a list of people who help you with your life challenges.

Try to add the people who are supportive of you, even if they aren't medical professionals..

The special doctors who have helped Jordyn! They are my medical detectives who always find a way to help me!

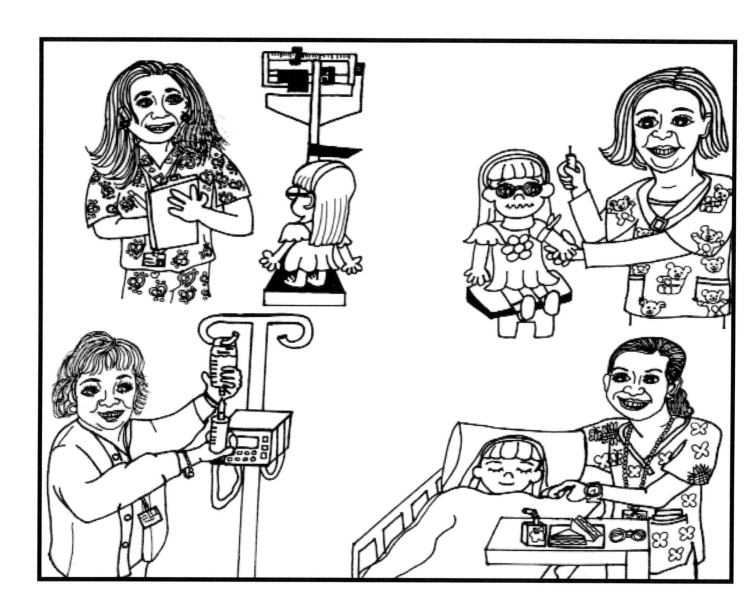

This is dedicated to all the nurses for their hard work, compassion and love for their patients.

My Social Worker helping me not to be afraid. We can be thankful
for all of the special professionals who help us!

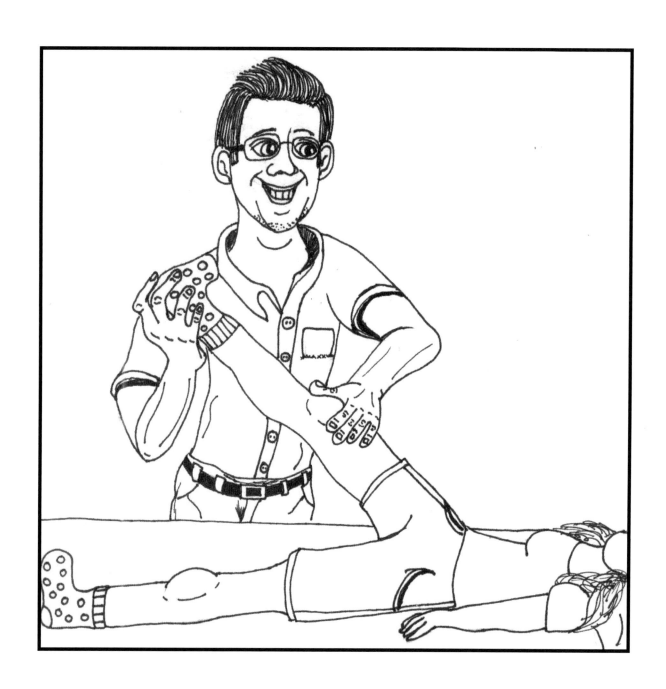

My Physical Therapist, more awesome professionals to help me regain strength and feel better.

A special doctor, my hematologist who helps my blood and body have greater energy to feel better!

Chapter 17:
Acknowledgements

Acknowledgements

I would like to dedicate this workbook to my marvelous niece, Jordyn Shapiro. You are a magnificent inspiration! Your ability to persevere, in spite of insurmountable obstacles, makes you a hero in my eyes and heart. Thank you my Jordyn Leigh, for the difference you make in my life.

Together, Jordyn and I wish to dedicate our workbook in memory of Hymie Hermele, AnaMae Shapiro-Pares and Daniel Shapiro. You will each forever be etched in our hearts and souls.

I thank my husband, John Comenzo, for the endless hours you encouraged me. The countless times you overlooked the missed dinners and keeping faith for the completion of this book! "I love you more!"

To Jodi, for the hours of labor and love you put into typing until our goal was reached. You're never ending patience, willingness to meet and edit has helped make my dream come true.
I love you, Jodi.

Jordyn wants to express her never ending love and gratitude to her Mom, Dad, Grandma Dorothy and sister Skylar. "You have each carried me through this journey. Stood by my side, no matter how difficult that became and believed in my healing, in spite of all of the signs indicating that I would never improve."

*Dr. Melvyn Grovit and Dr. Alfred Slonim, no words can express...
I truly don't know where I would be today had you not believed in me
and my quest to have a healthier quality of life. I love you both and
Thank God for you two daily!*

A special thank you to Dr. Ernie Eisenberg, chiropractor and staff
for helping complete the circle for my journey to wellness. I walk
taller, straighter and pain free because of your magic! Love, Jordyn

To my Aunt Maurie who has always been there for me! The past
two years were difficult health years but having my artwork with
this book helped me channel my emotions and was healing.
These drawings became a reflection of my inner feelings and
positive creativity.

As my mom likes to say, "A lot can happen in 24 hours so don't give
up hope."

You never gave up hope that I would get better. Thank you for
allowing me to use my journey to help people living daily with
illness to not give up hope! I love you! Jordyn

To my good friend Tristan Villanueva, for helping us arrange,
layout, and organize this book; without you, this book would not
exist! Check out the work at his website:
www.tristanmultimediaservice.com

To all of you who are working on this workbook; please remember…
You are never alone. We are in it together!
We keep standing strong with each other…Heart 2 Heart!

Dr. Maurie Comenzo and Jordyn Shapiro

Extra Workbook Pages

Made in the USA
Charleston, SC
13 June 2014